D1649183

GEORGE M. WHEELER

Wheeler's Photographic Survey of the American West, 1871-1873

WITH 50 LANDSCAPE PHOTOGRAPHS
by TIMOTHY O'SULLIVAN *and* WILLIAM BELL

DOVER PUBLICATIONS, INC., NEW YORK

Published in Canada by General Publishing Company, Ltd., 30 Lesmill Road, Don Mills, Toronto, Ontario.
Published in the United Kingdom by Constable and Company, Ltd., 10 Orange Street, London WC2H 7EG.

Wheeler's Photographic Survey of the American West, 1871–1873: With 50 Landscape Photographs by Timothy O'Sullivan and William Bell reproduces all of the photographs, with the original captions, contained in *Photographs Showing Landscapes, Geological and Other Features, of Portions of the Western Territory of the United States, Obtained in Connection with Geographical and Geological Explorations and Surveys West of the 100th Meridian (Seasons of 1871, 1872 and 1873)*, prepared under the direction of 1st Lieut. Geo. M. Wheeler, Corps of Engineers, U.S. Army, and originally published by the War Department, Washington, D.C., in 1875. The Publisher's Note, which was prepared specially for the present edition, is greatly indebted to James D. Horan's book *Timothy O'Sullivan: America's Forgotten Photographer.*

The publisher gratefully acknowledges the cooperation of Janet Lehr, of New York City, for lending the rare original album from which this book was directly reproduced.

Manufactured in the United States of America
Dover Publications, Inc., 180 Varick Street, New York, N.Y. 10014

Library of Congress Cataloging in Publication Data

O'Sullivan, Timothy H.
Wheeler's photographic survey of the American West, 1871–1873.

Originally published: Photographs showing landscapes, geological, and other features of portions of the western territory of the United States, obtained in connection with geographical and geological explorations and surveys west of the 100th meridian, seasons of 1871, 1872, and 1873. [Washington, D.C.]: War Dept., Corps of Engineers, U.S. Army, [1875]
The U.S. Geographical Surveys West of the 100th Meridian were under the direction of George M. Wheeler.
1. West (U.S.)—Description and travel—Views. 2. Southwest, New—Description and travel—Views. I. Wheeler, George M. (George Montague), 1842–1905. II. Bell, William. III. Geographical Surveys West of the 100th Meridian (U.S.) IV. Title. V. Title: Photographic survey of the American West.
F594.086 1983 978'.02 82-19773
ISBN 0-486-24466-0

PUBLISHER'S NOTE

"In the hands of Mr. O'Sullivan . . ., a little less than 300 negatives have been produced, illustrating the general appearance of the country, the mining districts, certain geological views, and a full and characteristic representation of that very grand and peculiar scenery among the cañons of the Colorado; a more unique series has hardly been produced in this country."

So wrote First Lieutenant George Montague Wheeler of the Army Corps of Engineers in a preliminary report on the 1871 season of the Geographical and Geological Explorations and Surveys West of the One Hundredth Meridian.

The fifty photographs in the present collection, taken by Timothy O'Sullivan and William Bell, are reproduced here from a rare album of original albumen prints hand-assembled in 1875 in a limited number of copies to supplement the seven-volume final report of the Wheeler survey. (The published report was illustrated with lithographed renderings of the photos.) In the original album, the prints were presented in three suites. The photographs from the 1871 season (all by O'Sullivan) were numbered 1–16; those from the second season (all by Bell) were numbered 1–15; and those taken in 1873 (all by O'Sullivan) were numbered 1–19. Here the photographs appear in their original sequence, but are numbered consecutively in the captions from 1 to 50. The numbers within parentheses in the captions represent the suite (I = 1871, II = 1872, III = 1873) and the original numbering within the suites; thus, our "50 (III, 19)" means "Dover illustration 50, which was the 19th of the 1873 suite." (The numbers scratched into light areas of each image probably represent the position of each photograph in the more extensive series from which these fifty were selected in 1875.)

The photographers of this period generally used the collodion or wet-plate process. Preparation of a negative involved coating a sheet of glass with collodion, a viscous solution of gun-cotton in ether and alcohol plus soluble iodine compounds. This sticky mixture, remaining on the plate after the solvents evaporated, became the vehicle for the light-sensitive silver iodide that precipitated onto the surface after a bath in silver nitrate. The plate had to be used while still wet, lest the emulsion lose its photosensitivity, so the photographer was obliged to move quickly from the "dark tent," a mobile laboratory mounted atop a wagon bed, to the camera. There the plate was exposed for ten seconds or so, and then rushed back to the tent to be developed and fixed. The entire process was so subject to the vagaries of weather and movement that it is remarkable that so many successful images were obtained by this means under primitive field conditions.

The area surveyed by Wheeler's team lies considerably to the west of the 100th meridian, which nearly bisects the continent in a line that passes just east of Dodge City, Kansas. During the seasons of 1871, 1872 and 1873, the expedition covered portions of the modern states of Arizona, California, Nevada, New Mexico and Utah. The sketch map on pages viii and ix shows the location of all but two of the features named in the photo captions (the spellings and boundary lines shown are the current ones). The areas within dotted and dashed lines delineate the sections that were mapped during each of the three seasons of the survey. Several of the pictures in the third suite (plates 32–50) show places outside the area covered in 1873; these were taken on side trips.

Before the Civil War, the U.S. government initiated systematic exploration of the territories that had been Mexican until the war of 1846–1848. The early surveys focused on topography, with the aim of identifying routes for travel between the settled Atlantic and Pacific coasts. The vision of a rail link between the East and California, realized in 1869, was already widely held in the prewar period. Photography played a role in the early expeditions. In *Photography and the American Scene* (Dover, 1964, 21201-7), Robert A. Taft recounts the experience of S. N. Carvalho, a daguerreotypist who accompanied Colonel Robert C. Frémont across the Great Divide in 1853. It seems that Frémont (later a candidate for President) got the idea of using the camera to document exploration from the writings of Alexander von Humboldt. Carvalho succeeded in making a photographic record of the expedition, but his plates were lost and the report they were to have illustrated (in lithographed renderings) was never published. Other attempts to use photography in ante-bellum Western exploration met with "indifferent success," due, in Taft's view, to technical deficiencies in the processes then in use and to the operators' lack of field experience.

After the Civil War, as the westward thrust of national destiny regained momentum, government-sponsored surveying of the frontier was resumed with zeal. The first large-scale survey, begun in 1867 under the direction of Clarence King, a civilian geologist, covered the region along the 40th parallel of latitude between the Rockies and the Sierra Nevada. King's party included the photographer Timothy O'Sullivan in addition to topographers, geologists, naturalists and cavalrymen. The next two surveys, headed by the noted earth scientists Ferdinand Vandiveer Hayden (1829–1887) and John Wesley Powell (1834–1902), respectively, continued to focus on geological considerations.

The survey that produced the photographs in this book was led by George M. Wheeler, a native of Hopkinton, Massachusetts. Born in 1842, Wheeler began his career in topographical engineering in 1867, just a year after graduating from West Point. His early reconnaissance work in Nevada and Utah convinced him of the need for a new survey, comparable in scale to those of King, Hayden and Powell, but different in emphasis. Wheeler proposed to chart "astronomical, geographical, and topographical observations, artificial and economic features, the geologic and natural history branches being treated as incidental to the main purpose." The information to be gathered would have not only military value with respect to the coming wars of extermination against the Southwestern Indians, but would also form the basis of a broad assessment of the region's potential for eventual economic exploitation.

Wheeler's proposal met a favorable reception in Washington, where the military command was intent on recovering a share of the now scanty appropriations for the surveying activities that had been its responsibility before the war. The Army's hidden agenda, carried out by a journalist ostensibly hired as a barometric observer and recorder, was to publicize the survey's findings in the popular press with the hope of strengthening Congressional support for funding of further military surveys in the postwar era of severe retrenchment. Wheeler apparently viewed photography more as a means of dramatizing the expedition's work than as a scientific tool in its own right. The photographer he chose was, in the later estimation of the famed frontier cameraman William Henry Jackson (quoted by Taft), "one of the best of the government photographers."

Timothy O'Sullivan was born around 1840, probably in Ireland. Little is known of his early life on Staten Island, New York. As a teenager, he apprenticed himself to Mathew B. Brady, one of the outstanding American photographers of the nineteenth century. (Brady's life and works are chronicled in Roy Meredith's *Mr. Lincoln's Camera Man* [Dover, 1964, 23021-X]). Brady had learned daguerreotypy from Samuel F. B. Morse, who was introduced to the new craft by its inventor, Louis-Jacques-Mandé Daguerre, in 1839. O'Sullivan practiced commercial portraiture for several years during the late 1850s, first in Brady's famous New York studio and later in Washington under the direction of Alexander Gardner.

When the Civil War broke out in 1861, O'Sullivan joined Brady's semiofficial photographic corps. He gained valuable experience in outdoor photography on the battlefields from Second Manassas to Appomattox, narrowly escaping death on at least two occasions. Although Brady and Gardner are often given credit for the powerful images of the conflict, O'Sullivan took many of the pictures, including nearly half of the views in Gardner's *Photographic Sketchbook of the Civil War* (Dover edition, 1959, 22731-6).

The expeditionary phase of O'Sullivan's professional life began in 1867 with the King survey mentioned above. The photographer spent three years tramping across the Great Basin and its environs, taking pictures that reflect the scientific and esthetic preoccupations of the expedition leader. King had a high opinion of the documentary value of photography in geological field work, and apparently hoped that the visual evidence recorded by O'Sullivan's camera would bolster the geological theories then in vogue. O'Sullivan made a series of interior views of the Comstock lode for the King survey—the first photographs of the inside of a mine ever taken in America. In 1870, Lieutenant Commander Thomas O. Selfridge of the U.S. Navy hired him as official photographer for an expedition to the Isthmus of Darién (now Panama, then part of Colombia) to map out a possible canal route.

O'Sullivan, by then a seasoned trekker, was one of the first men Wheeler selected for the surveys west of the 100th meridian in 1871. The photographer's salary of $150 a month was on a par with those of the junior scientists in the party. The costs of photographic equipment and supplies, borne by the Government, came to fully one-tenth of the first season's budget. O'Sullivan's outfit included a military ambulance that served as a mobile laboratory, several cameras and lenses, a patent developing box, glass for plates and an ample stock of chemicals.

In May 1871, Wheeler's team of soldiers, scientists, mule skinners, packers, laborers and guides assembled at Fort Halleck, Nevada. They headed south toward Death Valley, where the extreme heat made O'Sullivan's chemicals boil over. One man died in the desert, the first of several tragedies that would beset the expedition. A melodramatic incident of the summer was the disappearance of two civilian guides. Local newspapermen accused Wheeler of callous neglect, a charge he was later able to refute.

One of the most exciting episodes of that first season in the field was the ascent of the Colorado River from Camp Mohave on the California/Nevada line to Diamond Creek in the Grand Canyon, a distance of some 260 miles on some of the roughest water on the continent. Wheeler rationalized the mission (one of dubious scientific value, for others had previously made the journey) as necessary to test the limits of practical navigation. About 35 men boarded the flat-bottomed boats—perilous craft indeed compared with the rubber rafts that carry today's sportsmen in relative comfort and safety—and began to wend their way upstream.

O'Sullivan was in charge of the second boat, which he fittingly dubbed *The Picture.* During more than a month of grueling travel, the photographer managed, in Wheeler's words, "in the face of all obstacles, [to make] negatives at all available points." Time and again, O'Sullivan dragged his heavy equipment up sheer cliffs to capture the unforgettable scenery. In addition to the ceaseless work of his craft, O'Sullivan did his share of the rowing, pushing, portaging and packing. After one disastrous spill, he plunged into the swirling eddies in a vain attempt to recover the supplies and records swept overboard. For long stretches, the boats had to be pulled like barges on a canal—back-breaking labor made inconceivably exhausting by the unpredictable currents and the constant danger of ropes being cut by sharp rocks. The combined effects of injuries, dwindling rations and alternating periods of high stress and numbing depression took their toll on the men, nearly half of whom turned back midway upriver.

The remaining stalwarts pressed on, finally reaching the mouth of Diamond Creek where they were to rendezvous with an overland party. Wheeler ordered some of the men to march back to the base camp; the rest, including O'Sullivan, descended through the gorges by boat. Laden as the vessels were, the return trip took only five days and the carefully stowed cargo of glass negatives arrived intact. Winter was closing in, so Wheeler ended the year's work and sent O'Sullivan and the journalist Frederick Loring back to Washington to make the case, with words and pictures, that Congress should fund military, rather than civilian, surveys in the future. Ironically, many of the photographs that had survived the rigorous journey up and down the wild river were lost en route. Loring was killed when his stagecoach was ambushed, but O'Sullivan, following a different route, made it to the East. Upon his return to the frontier, he was temporarily reassigned to another survey with his old colleague Clarence King.

The extant views taken in 1871, reproduced here on plates 1–16, show the pristine beauty of the canyon country. The surface of the Colorado River appears deceptively placid in these photographs, an illusion created by the long exposure of the negatives. Not all the vantage points O'Sullivan used are accessible today. The construction of Hoover Dam in 1936 submerged portions of the Colorado gorge under the waters of Lake Mead.

For the 1872 season, O'Sullivan was replaced by William Bell, who is variously identified as a Philadelphian or as an Englishman. Some sources make him a physician; all agree that he was a skillful photographer. Robert Taft (*op. cit.*) points out that Bell, unlike most of the expeditionary photographers of this period, used a dry process that involved bathing the collodion-coated plate in a tannic-acid solution and then drying it in the dark. The additional step made it possible to store prepared plates for fairly long periods, which could not be done with wet plates. However, the dry plates required much longer exposure time than the wet ones did.

O'Sullivan resumed work with the Wheeler survey in 1873, the last year represented in this photographic collection. In recognition of O'Sullivan's previously demonstrated leadership ability, Wheeler gave him considerable executive responsibility during this season. His nonphotographic duties included the command of several field parties, the purchase of supplies and, by one account, the mediation of recurrent disputes between soldiers and civilians. Somehow the photographer found time to take some of his most memorable pictures. In addition to landscape vistas, he obtained views of sites important in the Indian and Spanish periods of the region's history: Inscription Rock, now in El Morro National Monument (Plates 39, 40 and 45); the White House ruins (Plate 41) in Canyon de Chelly (another National Monument also shown in Plates 46 and 47); the historic churches of Santa Fe (Plate 42) and Zuni (Plate 49); and the ancient Zuñi Pueblo (Plates 48 and 50).

The Wheeler survey continued for several more years, but 1875 was O'Sullivan's last year in the field. In 1879, he was appointed official photographer of the newly organized United States Geological Survey under Clarence King, but was essentially inactive. In 1880, he applied for the position of photographer in the Treasury Department with enthusiastic recommendations from many highly placed former colleagues. He served for only five months until his declining health forced him to retire to Staten Island, where he died of tuberculosis in 1882.

George Wheeler was promoted to captain in 1879. He was desk-bound for several years, preparing the voluminous survey reports. In 1881, he represented the United States at the third International Geographical Congress and Exhibition in Venice. The rigors of travel in the West had broken his health, and he went into semiretirement in 1883. He continued to write scientific reports until 1888, when he finally left the military service with the rank and pay of a major. Wheeler died in New York in 1905.

The Wheeler survey achieved its stated goals, to the extent that it mapped vast tracts of land and amassed volumes of scientific data. However, the establishment of the U.S. Geological Survey within the Department of the Interior effectively ended the struggle between civilian and military agencies for the control of future surveying and exploration. The Army Corps of Engineers, though deprived of its surveying functions, continued to make its mark on the American landscape. The survey's photographs of the majestic Western wilderness endure as historic documents and as powerful artistic images.

NOTES ON THE CAPTIONS

While a detailed discussion of the geography, geology, natural history and ethnography of the region depicted in the photographs is beyond the scope of this essay, a few definitions of terms in the captions are in order. For this publication, the captions from the printed mounts in the album have been reset, but the original wording and spelling conventions have been retained: cañon for canyon, Chelle for Chell(e)y, Pahute for Paiute, Navajoe for Navaho, Sheavwitz for Shivwits, Zuni for Zuñi. The Colorado tributary called Paria Creek appears in modern atlases as the Paria River.

The term "wash" refers either to the dry bed of an intermittent stream, typically at the bottom of a canyon, or to the mound of rubble that spreads in fan-shaped, corrugated slopes below a gash in a cliff. "Rhyolite" is a type of volcanic rock related to granite. *Cereus giganteus* (now officially called *Carnegiea gigantea*) is the saguaro or giant cactus (the state flower of Arizona), a species that can attain a height of fifty feet. The "park" of Cooley's Park (Plate 36) refers to a natural formation of grassland with scattered trees, usually in a level valley, and does not necessarily imply human alteration of the landscape.

The Spanish inscriptions in plates 39 and 40 contain many abbreviations and old or unacademic spellings. The one on plate 39 reads: "Aqui estuvo el Genl D^{n} D^{o} de Varg^{s} q^{n} conquisto a nrã S^{a} Fé, y a la R^{l} Corona todo el nuebo mexico a su costa Año D̄ 1692" (Here stood General Don Diego de Vargas, who conquered all of New Mexico at his own expense for our holy faith and for the royal crown, A.D. 1692). The one on plate 40 reads: "Por aqui pazo el Alferes D Joseph de Payba Basconzelos el año que trujo (?; tuvo?) el Cavildo del Reyno a su costa a 18 de feb° de 1526 Años" (The Ensign [municipal official] Don José de Paiba Vasconcelos passed by here the year he held [brought?] the council of the kingdom at his expense, February 18, 1526).

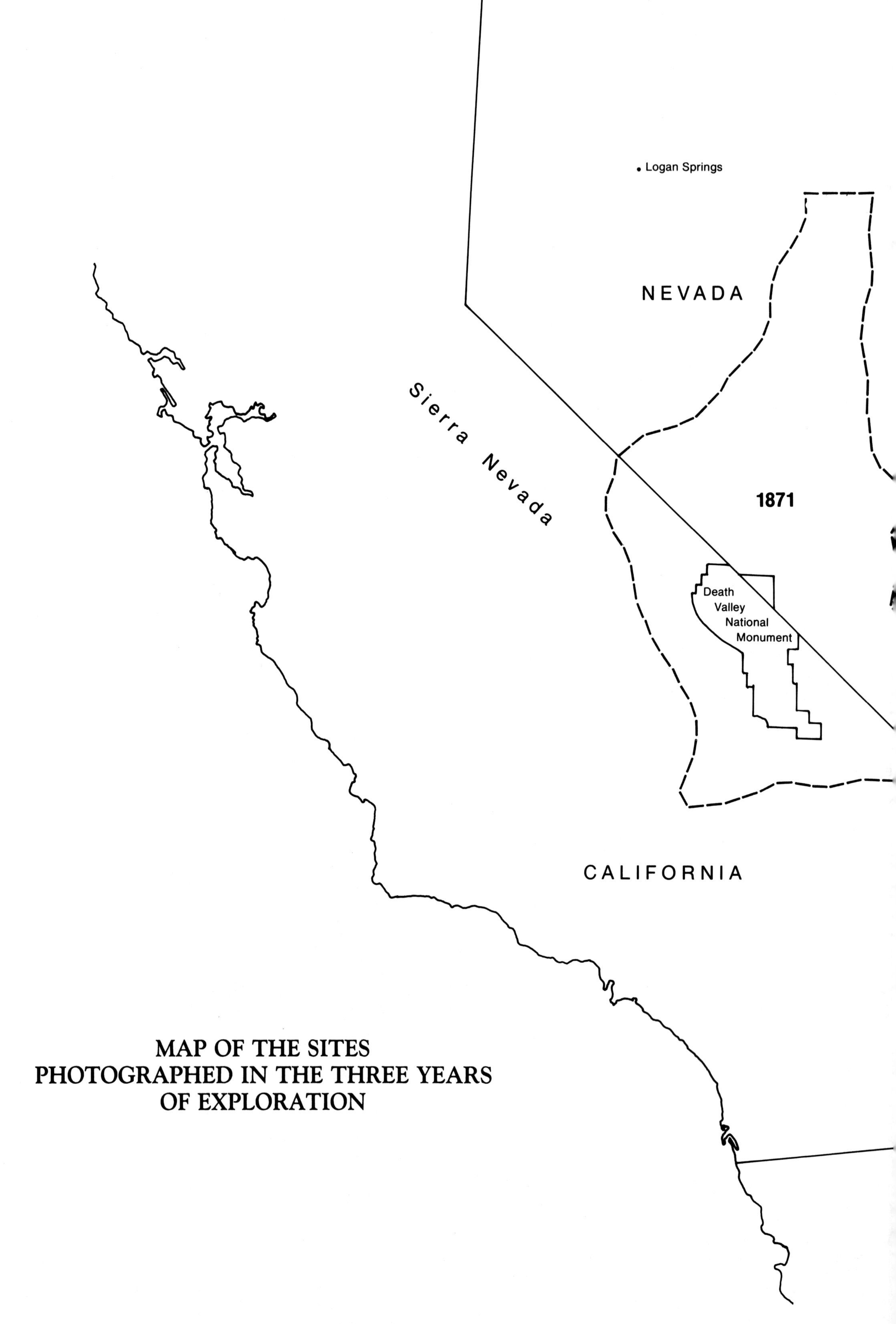

MAP OF THE SITES
PHOTOGRAPHED IN THE THREE YEARS
OF EXPLORATION

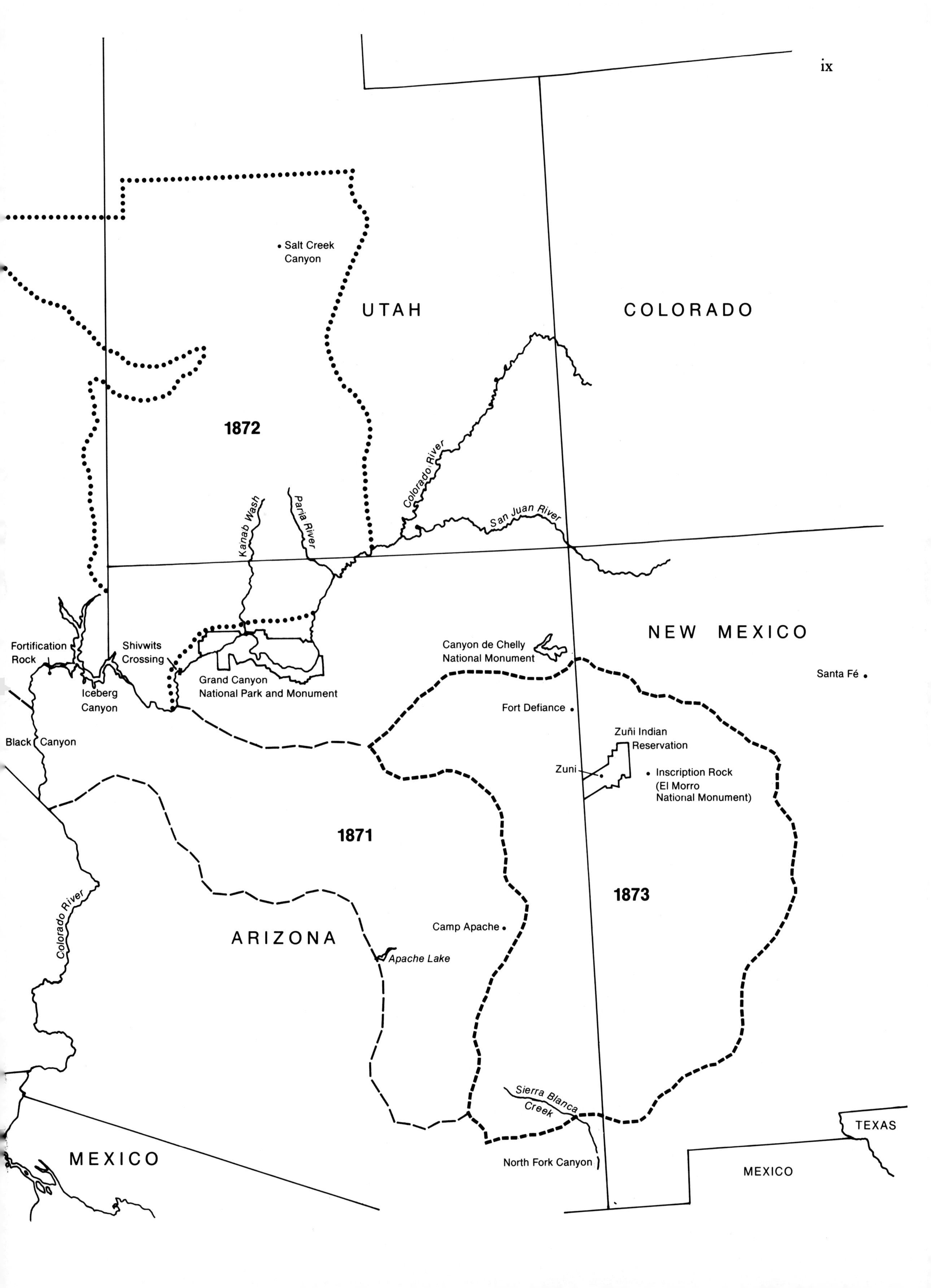
UTAH
COLORADO
NEW MEXICO
ARIZONA
MEXICO
TEXAS
MEXICO
1872
1871
1873
Salt Creek Canyon
Colorado River
San Juan River
Kanab Wash
Paria River
Fortification Rock
Shivwits Crossing
Iceberg Canyon
Grand Canyon National Park and Monument
Black Canyon
Canyon de Chelly National Monument
Santa Fé
Fort Defiance
Zuñi Indian Reservation
Zuni
Inscription Rock (El Morro National Monument)
Camp Apache
Apache Lake
Colorado River
Sierra Blanca Creek
North Fork Canyon

Opposite: Original title page of the Wheeler album.

PHOTOGRAPHS

SHOWING

LANDSCAPES, GEOLOGICAL AND OTHER FEATURES, OF PORTIONS

OF THE

WESTERN TERRITORY OF THE UNITED STATES,

OBTAINED IN CONNECTION WITH

Geographical and Geological

EXPLORATIONS AND SURVEYS

WEST OF THE 100TH MERIDIAN

SEASONS OF 1871, 1872 AND 1873.

1ST LIEUT GEO. M. WHEELER,

CORPS OF ENGINEERS, U.S. ARMY

IN CHARGE.

1 (I,1) Snow Peaks, Bull Run Mining District, Nevada.

2 (I,2) Group of Pah-Ute Indians, Nevada.

3 (I,3) Bluff Opposite Big Horn Camp, Black Cañon, Colorado River.

4 (I,4) Black Cañon, Colorado River, Looking Below from Big Horn Camp.

5 (I,5) Black Cañon, Colorado River, Looking Above from Camp 7.

6 (I,6) Black Cañon, Colorado River, Looking Below, Near Camp 7.

7 (I,7) Black Cañon, Colorado River, Looking Below Near Camp 7.

8 (I,8) Black Cañon, Colorado River, From Camp 8, Looking Above.

9 (I,9) Black Cañon, Colorado River, Looking Above from Mirror Bar.

10 (I,10) Entrance to Black Cañon, Colorado River from Above.

11 (I,11) Wall in the Grand Cañon, Colorado River.

12 (I,12) *Cereus giganteus,* Arizona.

13 (I,13) Water Rhyolites, Near Logan Springs, Nevada.

14 (I,14) Rock Carved by Drifting Sand, Below Fortification Rock, Arizona.

15 (I,15) Iceberg Cañon, Colorado River, Looking Above.

16 (I,16) Alpine Lake, in the Sierra Nevada, California.

17 (II,1) Cañon of Kanab Wash, Colorado River, Looking South.

18 (II,2) Cañon of Kanab Wash, Colorado River, Looking North.

19 (II,3) Cañon of Kanab Wash, Colorado River, Looking South.

20 (II,4) Cañon of Kanab Wash, Colorado River, Looking South.

21 (II,5) Colorado River, Mouth of Kanab Wash, Looking West.

22 (II,6) Grand Cañon, Colorado River, Near Paria Creek, Looking West.

23 (II,7) Grand Cañon, Colorado River, Near Paria Creek, Looking West.

24 (II,8) Grand Cañon, Colorado River, Near Paria Creek, Looking East.

25 (II,9) Looking South into the Grand Cañon, Colorado River. Sheavwitz Crossing.

26 (II,10) Rain Sculpture, Salt Creek Cañon, Utah.

27 (II,11) Grand Cañon of the Colorado River, Mouth of Kanab Wash, Looking West.

28 (II,12) Grand Cañon of the Colorado River, Mouth of Kanab Wash, Looking East.

29 (II,13) Grand Cañon of the Colorado River, Mouth of Kanab Wash, Looking West.

30 (II,14) Perched Rock, Rocker Creek, Arizona.

31 (II,15) Limestone Walls, Kanab Wash, Colorado River.

32 (III,1) Apache Lake, Sierra Blanca Range, Arizona.

33 (III,2) View on Apache Lake, Sierra Blanca Range, Arizona.

34 (III,3) View on Apache Lake, Sierra Blanca Range, Arizona. Two Apache Scouts in the foreground.

35 (III,4) North Fork Cañon, Sierra Blanca Creek, Arizona.

36 (III,5) Cooley's Park, Sierra Blanca Range, Arizona.

37 (III,6) Distant View of Camp Apache, Arizona.

38 (III,7) Aboriginal Life Among the Navajoe Indians. Near old Fort Defiance, N.M.

39 (III,8) Historic Spanish Record of the Conquest. South Side of Inscription Rock, N.M.

40 (III,9) Historic Spanish Record of the Conquest. South Side of Inscription Rock, N.M. No. 3.

41 (III,10) Ancient Ruins in the Cañon de Chelle, N.M. In a niche 50 feet above present Cañon bed.

42 (III,11) The Church of San Miguel. The oldest in Santa Fé, N.M.

43 (III,12) Looking Across the Colorado River to Mouth of Paria Creek.

44 (III,13) Cañon of the Colorado River, near Mouth of San Juan River, Arizona.

45 (III,14)   South Side of Inscription Rock, N.M.

46 (III,15) Cañon de Chelle. Walls of the Grand Cañon about 1200 feet in height.

47 (III,16) Head of Cañon de Chelle, Looking Down. Walls about 1200 feet in height.

48 (III,17) Indian Pueblo, Zuni, N.M. View from the South.

49 (III,18) Old Mission Church, Zuni Pueblo, N.M. View from the Plaza.

50 (III,19) Section of South Side of Zuni Pueblo, N.M.